YOU'RE TOAST

and Other Metaphors We Adore

by Nancy Loewen
illustrated by Donald Wu

PICTURE WINDOW BOOKS
a capstone imprint

What is a metaphor?

Editor: Jill Kalz
Designer: Lori Bye
Art Director: Nathan Gassman
Production Specialist: Michelle Biedscheid
The illustrations in this book were created digitally.

Picture Window Books
151 Good Counsel Drive
P.O. Box 669
Mankato, MN 56002-0669
877-845-8392
www.capstonepub.com

All books published by Picture Window Books are manufactured
with paper containing at least 10 percent post-consumer waste.

Library of Congress Cataloging-in-Publication Data
Loewen, Nancy, 1964-
   You're toast and other metaphors we adore / by Nancy Loewen ;
illustrated by Donald Wu.
      p. cm. — (Ways to say it)
   Includes index.
   ISBN 978-1-4048-6270-8 (library binding) — ISBN 978-1-4048-6717-8
(paperback)
   1. Metaphor—Juvenile literature. I. Wu, Donald, ill. II. Title.
   PE1445.M4L64 2011
   428.1—dc22
                                            2010033770

MAR 2 9 2012

Special thanks to our adviser, Terry Flaherty, PhD,
Professor of English, Minnesota State University, Mankato,
for his expertise.

Printed in the United States of America in North Mankato, Minnesota.
072011   006321VMI

A metaphor can be **crystal clear** or at the **end of its rope.**

It can be  a **PIG,**

a **peach,**

or a
can of worms.

A metaphor is a figure of speech that compares two things. These things are different, but they're also alike in at least one way. A metaphor shows what the two things have in common.

Don't be a **chicken!** Turn the page, and start learning about metaphors.

Meet Etta.

Meet Etta's brother, Cory.

Meet the last piece of Grandma Greta's HEAVENLY blueberry pie. It's OUT OF THIS WORLD!

The blueberries are as fat as Ping-Pong balls.

"Heavenly" and "out of this world" are metaphors. They tell us Grandma's pie is special.

Similes also compare two things. But similes use connecting words such as *like* or *as*. Metaphors don't. With metaphors, one thing *is* another. "As fat as Ping-Pong balls" is a simile. It uses the word *as* to compare the blueberries to Ping-Pong balls.

5

Etta **has her eye on** that pie.

She'd **give her right arm for it.**

So would Cory.

A lot of metaphors are idioms. Idioms don't make sense when we look at the actual meaning of the words. Etta's eye isn't really on the pie. She's just watching it closely. And neither Etta nor Cory wants to give up an arm! The saying just highlights how much the kids want the pie.

"Just cut it in half," Grandma says.

"I don't **see** that happening," says Cory.

Idioms are easy to spot. But common words are metaphors too. When Cory uses the word *see*, he means he doesn't think it will happen.

"If you won't share it, you'll have to win it," Grandma says. "First one to the mailbox and back gets the pie!"

Cory takes off.

Etta is right on his heels,

but Cory **wins by a nose.**

Metaphors make writing more colorful. Etta isn't really on Cory's heels—just very close. Cory barely wins the race. But does he win by the length of a nose? Probably not.

"Wins by a nose" is a horse-racing phrase that's been used since about 1900. A horse's nose is the first part of its body to cross the finish line.

"OK," Grandma says. "I'll spin you around, blindfolded, 20 times. Whoever falls first loses."

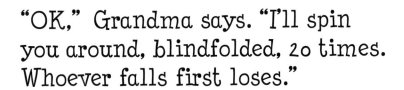

"piece of cake," says Etta.

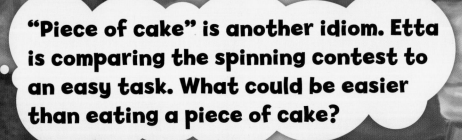

"Piece of cake" is another idiom. Etta is comparing the spinning contest to an easy task. What could be easier than eating a piece of cake?

But Cory wins that one too.

The saying "piece of cake" was first used by the Royal Air Force (United Kingdom) in the 1930s. It described an easy flight.

"Let's make it three out of five!"
Etta shouts.

"Fine with me," Cory says.

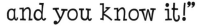

"YOU'RE TOAST, and you know it!"

When Cory tells Etta she's "toast", he's saying she doesn't have a chance of winning. She'll be scorched and served up to eat! Metaphors like this one are slang. Slang is language we use when we're talking to people in informal situations.

"I've hidden a spool of purple thread," Grandma says.
"Whoever finds it first wins."

Cory peeks under a chair.

"You're **cold**,"
Grandma says.

14

Etta looks behind some plants. "You're **warm**," Grandma says,

"and **getting warmer** ... You're **burning up!**"

"Got it!" Etta cries.

Here, "cold" means Cory is far away from the thread. "Warm" means Etta is close. It's like our solar system: The planets closest to the sun are much hotter than the ones far away.

Temperature words are used in a lot of metaphors. Here are a few examples: hot temper, cold trail, icy stare, cold shoulder, chill out, boil over, frozen with fear.

The next contest is a game of H-O-R-S-E.
Both kids make some shots and miss some shots.

"My, this game is a
NAIL BITER!"
Grandma exclaims.

Etta's final shot swishes through the net. Cory's shot bounces off the rim.

"I win!" Etta shouts.

"I'm on a roll now!"

Some people bite their fingernails when they can't relax. When Grandma calls the game a "nail-biter," she's excited about the close score.

When something is rolling, it's got energy. It's hard to stop. Etta is sure she'll win the next game too.

17

"The last contest is a word game," Grandma says. "See how many words you can make using the letters in BLUEBERRY PIE."

Cory and Etta

BUCKLE DOWN.

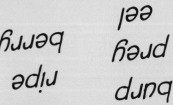

burp
prey
eel

ripe
berry

When Grandma says "**Time's up**," Cory has five words. Etta has seven.

"I win!" Etta cries. "The pie is mine!"

Some metaphors, such as "buckle down," are easy to picture. Cory and Etta are focused on the game. It's like they're buckled into their seats. "Time's up" is harder to see. When you think about it, what does "up" have to do with time?

The phrase "time is up" has been in use for at least 600 years.

beep
lip
blue
rib
bee
burr
rule

Oh, no!

"DAD!" Etta wails. Her face **CLOUDS OVER.**

Metaphors can be a quick way of getting an idea across. We know Etta had been very happy— a feeling we connect with a sunny day. Then she sees the pie is gone. She's not happy anymore. The clouds have moved in front of the sun.

21

"Oh, well," Grandma says. "We'll just make another pie. Together!"

"**Sweet!**" say Cory and Etta.

Many metaphors use words that connect to our senses. We enjoy things that taste sweet. Cory and Etta will enjoy making a pie—and eating it too!

Hopping Mad for Metaphors

Wouldn't it be fun if metaphors were really true? Here's an activity that will get you learning and laughing—and will draw out the artist in you as well.

The sentences below contain common metaphors that describe people. (The meanings follow.) Pick two or three metaphors from the list and draw a silly person to match!

He was all ears. (He listened carefully.)

She had a heart of gold. (She was a good, kind person.)

He wore rose-colored glasses. (He saw things in a positive way.)

She had a green thumb. (She was good at growing plants.)

She kept her fingers crossed. (She was hoping for something good to happen.)

He bit his tongue. (He didn't say anything.)

She was caught red-handed. (She was caught doing something wrong.)

He had something up his sleeve. (He had a secret idea or plan.)

She had ants in her pants. (She couldn't sit still.)

He buried his head in the sand. (He refused to do something about a problem.)

CHALLENGE: When you've finished your drawings, share them with your friends. See if they can guess the metaphors!

23

To Learn More

More Books to Read

Brennan-Nelson, Denise. *My Daddy Likes to Say.* Chelsea, Mich.: Sleeping Bear Press, 2009.

Cleary, Brian P. *Skin Like Milk, Hair of Silk: What Are Similes and Metaphors?* Words Are CATegorical. Minneapolis: Millbrook Press, 2009.

Heinrichs, Ann. *Similes and Metaphors.* The Magic of Language. Chanhassen, Minn.: Child's World, 2006.

Herman, Gail. *Snowboarding Similes and Metaphors.* Grammar All-Stars. Pleasantville, N.Y.: Gareth Stevens Pub., 2009.

Internet Sites

FactHound offers a safe, fun way to find Internet sites related to this book. All of the sites on FactHound have been researched by our staff.

Here's all you do:
Visit *www.facthound.com*
Type in this code: 9781404862708

Check out projects, games and lots more at
www.capstonekids.com

Glossary

compare—to look closely at things to discover ways they are alike or different

figure of speech—a word or words that create an effect without using their real meaning; a metaphor is a figure of speech

idiom—a common saying or expression that is special to a language or culture

metaphor—a figure of speech that compares different things without using connecting words such as *like* or *as*

phrase—a group of words that are used together

simile—a figure of speech that compares different things using *like* or *as*

slang—informal speech

Index

Look for all the books in the Ways to Say It series:

She Sells Seashells and Other Tricky Tongue Twisters
Stubborn as a Mule and Other Silly Similes
Talking Turkey and Other Clichés We Say
You're Toast and Other Metaphors We Adore